xuāi
mission, house, village, town

xuāi
mission, house, village, town

Lisa Kay Adam

Copyright © 2018 Lisa Kay Adam
All Rights Reserved
Manufactured in the United States

ISBN: 978-1-942956-46-4
Library of Congress Control Number: 2018942367

Thanks to Mapoteca Manuel Orozco y Berra and Servicio de Informacíon Agroalimentaria y Pesquera (SAGARPA), Mexico, for permission to use the 1744 map, *Mapa de la nueva provincia poblada de bárbaros.*

Lamar University Literary Press
Beaumont, Texas

Dedicated to
those who came before us

Recent Poetry from Lamar University Literary Press

Bobby Aldridge, *An Affair of the Stilled Heart*
Michael Baldwin, *Lone Star Heart, Poems of a Life in Texas*
Charles Behlen, *Failing Heaven*
Alan Berecka, *With Our Baggage*
David Bowles, *Flower, Song, Dance: Aztec and Mayan Poetry*
Jerry Bradley, *Crownfeathers and Effigies*
Jerry Bradley and Ulf Kirchdorfer, editors, *The Great American Wise Ass Poetry Anthology*
Matthew Brennan, *One Life*
Mark Busby, *Through Our Times*
Paul Christensen, *The Jack of Diamonds is a Hard Card to Play*
Stan Crawford, *Resisting Gravity*
Chip Dameron, *Waiting for an Etcher*
Glover Davis, *My Cap of Darkness*
William Virgil Davis, *The Bones Poems*
Jeffrey DeLotto, *Voices Writ in Sand*
Chris Ellery, *Elder Tree*
Mimi Ferebee, *Wildfires and Atmospheric Memories*
Larry Griffin, *Cedar Plums*
Ken Hada, *Margaritas and Redfish*
Katherine Hoerth, *Goddess Wears Cowboy Boots*
Michael, Jennings, *An Affair of the Stilled Heart*
Lynn Hoggard, *Motherland: Stories and Poems of Louisiana*
Gretchen Johnson, *A Trip Through Downer, Minnesota*
Ulf Kirchdorfer, *Chewing Green Leaves*
Laozi, *Daodejing*, tr. By David Breeden, Steven Schroeder, and Wally Swist
Janet McCann, *The Crone at the Casino*
Jim McGarrah, *The Truth About Mangoes*
J. Pittman McGehee, *Extraordinary in the Ordinary*
Laurence Musgrove, *Local Bird*
Godspower Oboido, *Wandering Feet of Pebbled Shores*
Dave Oliphant, *The Pilgrimage*
Carol Coffee Reposa, *Underground Musicians*
Jan Seale, *The Parkinson Poems*
Steven Schroeder, *the moon, not the finger, pointing*
Carol Smallwood, *Water, Earth, Air, Fire, and Picket Fences*
Glen Sorestad *Hazards of Eden*
W.K. Stratton, *Ranchero Ford/ Dying in Red Dirt Country*
Loretta Diane Walker, *Desert Light*
Wally Swist, *Invocation*
Jonas Zdanys (ed.), *Pushing the Envelope, Epistolary Poems*
Jonas Zdanys, *Red Stones*
Jonas Zdanys, *Three White Horses*

Acknowledgments

The unflagging encouragement of Jan Seale, the 2012 Texas Poet Laureate, helped bring these poems to print. I'm deeply grateful for her support, and thankful that she directed me to Lamar University Literary Press. Likewise, I'm so thankful for old friends, too numerous to name, who have supported me in countless ways, and for new friends at San Miguel Poetry Week who have welcomed me into the fold of writers.

I can scarcely number the many teachers I am indebted to, but I am most grateful for the generous spirits of Olga Paul and Dr. Miles Richardson, who encouraged open-hearted exploration of the world through writing. I've also been fortunate to work in the field of museums, which are pathways to lifelong learning, and for that I'm grateful to the Museum of South Texas History and other museums where I have worked or volunteered. Above all, I owe unbounded gratitude to my parents, Red and Max Adam.

CONTENTS

I. *masō, kuāx, wāyo*
- 13   They are few
  Oxtcīxupā
- 15   *Nakāwanō*
  I love God alone
- 17   With all my heart
  Naxasāl auxyokuēn
- 19   *Anikuēkat Dios tupō osō ē?*
  Where is God?
- 21   *Niwakuāntzam axām kalomē*
  If perchance I do not die
- 23   When the world comes to an end
  Tap pa akuē apāxāi tukuēt
- 25   This is going to come to pass
  Ampakāl san apām

II. *nāko, xt'ēwal, tālam*
- 29   In this world
  Tap pa akuēt
- 31   Have you made fun of them?
  Mamīkaxāmayasauxuam ē?
- 32   Twice twenty and ten
  Taiwakō axtē ko xūyopamāux axtē
- 34   My soul
  Napāxam
- 35   Words
  Pilāpaxlē
- 37   *Naxopimāma*
  Our Father
- 39   He will cast them into hell
  T'oaxām tukuēt akpahākoxt'ām sanpō
- 41   I am worth nothing
  Pīntci nakāmmam axām
- 43   Witch
  Yēwal

III. *hōi, malkūita, tānko*
- 47   What is your name?
  T'āhaka xaxauxuē ?
- 49   Have you danced the mitote?
  Txē mamaixā yam ē?
- 51   *Mamāyayūnayām ē ?*
  Did you fast?
- 53   Do not be ashamed before me
  Tiaxuānkam axām kām
- 56   For how many years have you been sinning with this woman?
  T'āxat āxakō aptcīka tāgu pitapōyō saxpām pinapsā mahōi salatē?

57	Have you lived in concubinage with any man?	
	Xak'āu mām ē?	
58	Have you been angry with some man?	
	Mamayāxt'ēgulo yam ē?	
59	*Xakuātzum ē?*	
	Did you pardon this man?	
60	How many people are there?	
	T'āxat apsākapā?	
63	God commands	
	Dios po watānko	
IV.	*xāmtzam, tzakēx, saayēx, mi*	
67	He has come to visit you	
	Mamāk kamām tcon	
69	She was shut in	
	Apot'āwaxōpē	
71	Those who wish to marry	
	Ax xek'ātzawamkē tapamō axpam	
73	Do you really desire to marry?	
	Mak xanayē xamīn pil' mameyak'āu atāpamo kalō yam ē ?	
75	Did you steal anything?	
	Pin pil' mā xōuxtcā'akē xō ē?	
78	I am very much pleased	
	Tzin nikāwa sāux pam	
80	All the things the priests have taught me	
	Kutātze tupā takpaxātzo wakō tutcēn	
V.	*mestīa, kuām, spāmo, kāwa*	
85	We will speak to God	
	Dios tupōm niyolātze wakō kam	
86	Are you a witch?	
	Xapakuāxo ē?	
88	I hope	
	Nakuām	
90	God will pardon you	
	Dios tupō makpakuātzum san tupāyō	
92	I believe it	
	Naspāmo	
94	Because you love me much	
	Taxakāwa pam inō	
97	Be joyful!	
	Xikāwa sāux!	
VI.	*wamalēt*	
101	All the dead	
	Apaxumātz tupāt	
103	Finding Pieces of the Coahuiltecan World in Words from the Past	

I.

masō
to give up
to abandon
to leave
to desert

kuāx
to suffer

wāyo
to cry (as an animal)
to howl
to weep

They are few
Oxtcīxupā

I will tell you how it was in those days,
when the strangers first came to this land.
At first we thought to ourselves, humph,
oxtcīxupā, they are few.
We will harass them
the way a flock of blackbirds
mobs a hawk. But then we saw, no!
Oxāuxuipā! They are many!
From the mountains to the south
they came, more and more,
the way hawk after hawk
comes out of the woods
on the warm afternoon air.

But still this did not alarm us.
We had been in this land since the beginning.
We had learned that all beings wax and wane.
The silver berry of the moon is eaten and grows again.
The season of burning sun gives way to blowing cold.
The long times of drought change to rain.
Even the animals have their long circles.
The rabbit, the speckled quail,
they increase and decrease in numbers,
the same as the animals who eat them.

And now in these days, it seems the strangers,
and all who are with them, grow like the waxing moon.
Their people, their hungry herds of animals,
even the small mice that live among them,
and our own white-winged doves who flock
to their fields when the seeds are sown—
oxāuxuipā, they are many.

Yet the deer and the spotted cat hide in the woods,
as we hunt them to satisfy the endless hunger
of the strangers for their skins. The tall grass
is trampled and grows thin under the hungry
mouths of horse and cow and sheep.
And our people?
They are scattered or diminished.
The old, the young, and the weak
die from disease, or despair.
How many still speak our tongue,
who can I tell this story to?
Oxtcīxupā, there are few.

When will the long circle turn?
When will our favorable moon return?

Nakāwanō
I love God alone

This is the truth, *mantpām pāx*,
for who else would I love?

Grandmother, *kāka*, first among my family
to love me, first to die among our people
from the rash that swarmed her body like ants.
Mother, *lēic,* father, *t'ānagē*—dead,
burned to death from the red rash.
Younger sister, *tzūtzan—*
oh small child, you raised your head
just once when I called your name,
then closed your eyes forever.
I myself folded you in palm matting,
scraped back the soil with my digging stick,
placed my conch shell pendant around your neck,
felt your head nod like a sunflower on its thin stalk.

Alone, I came here, where the priests
told me of their god, urged me,
Miakāwa pām kam, you are to love him.

Grandmother! Mother! Father!
I cried to you—*Taxtāgex!* Aid me!
And you did not help me.

I came here, alone, and the priests urged me,
Miakāwa pām kam, you are to love him.

I came here and found the enemies
of my people, collected here also,
each of us in our calamities.

The priests urge me,
Miakāwa pām kam, you are to love him.

I am so alone.
Who else is there to love?
I cry out, *Nakāwanō!*
I love God alone!

With all my heart
Naxasāl auxyokuēn

I have been one who answered life
with all my heart, *naxasāl auxyokuēn*,
and who led others with my heart,
who always answered yes, first.

When the priests told us—
Xuāi pitakuēm mamāimasō snex,
you should abandon this place,
I was the first to gather
baskets and hides and children,
and other women followed me,
and husbands went with wives.

We women worked like a flock
of flitting swallows to build new homes
clustered around the mission. Like swallows,
we gathered the mud and sticks
to daub on poles the men had set.
Like swallows we gathered grasses
for our roofs, and as we gathered,
we sang happily as swallows sing.

But now I see that birds are wiser.
No swallow builds a nest in a place
that will be destroyed by storm,
or builds a nest in a place of pestilence.

Our homes were washed away by flood.
With all my heart, *naxasāl auxyokuēn,*
I cried. With all my heart, and my voice,
I stirred our people to build again.

But for what? To see
our new children stillborn, to see
our young children die of fever,
our old children leave us
to marry strangers?

More than one of our mud homes
stands empty now. No families
will return to them next year.
There will be no happy singing
filling them next year.

Now I am afraid for others
to follow my yes or no.
But something in my heart tells me—
Xuāi pitakuēm mamāimasō snex,
you should abandon this place.

Anikuēkat Dios tupō osō ē?
Where is God?

When the priests ask this,
the answer wanted is—
in the little pieces of bread, *ax xuīzkuan,*
or in the church, or in heaven.
Anikuēkat Dios tupō osō ē?
Where is God?

I do not care where God is!
In such small or far-away places!

Where am I?
This is what I ask myself.
Most days I walk only from the mission
to the fields and back,
but I am lost. I look around

and no thing speaks to me,
nothing tells me where I am.
All that is around me—
the walls, the doors, the tools,
the fool trinkets given to the women,
the piles and boxes on all sides,
and more that arrive each day it seems—
all these things are mute.
They have use, but they are
as mute as the dead.

Never was I lost before.
Even if I strayed from the hunt
or sought a solitary spot
beneath the deepest shade of an ebony,
then around me still were the animals and plants,

each with its true name and energy.
Each spoke to me of its worth,
each told me I was home,
each led me home, as surely
as the summer wind told me which way is south.
And like the plants, I too grew
in my place, I lived among the living.
Uprooted, now I dwell
amid the dead things.

Anikuēkat Dios tupō osō ē?
Where is God?

I do not care!

Niwakuāntzam axām kalomē
If perchance I do not die

From my sick bed I watch
the dust motes dance in the sliver
of sunlight. They seem
more alive than me.
They stir my thoughts.
I know that, if I live, I should
again take up the plow,
again say my prayers,
give thanks for healing.
I should, but—
if perchance I do not die,
niwakuāntzam axām kalomē—
I want to go back.
I don't want to live or die, anymore,
in these close, pestilent rooms
of shadow and smoke.
I want to go back
to the ways of our fathers,
the woods of our grandfathers.

I want to go back. I can.
I know I'm getting better. My body is warmer today.
My vision is not so dim as yesterday.
Yes, today I see as clearly as a day in winter
when the sun smiles from behind clouds.
Today I hear so well the loud rattles
of the grey cranes flying south,
and I want to fly away, too!
The strength in my limbs
is returning, I feel it. I believe
I could make the walk
to find those who fled

instead of coming to this
lost place.

Niwakuāntzam axām kalomē,
if perchance I do not die—
hunger would not mean much,
and I would like to walk and walk and walk again,
freely, and feel the snap of the bowstring,
throw loud shouts to the long winds.

The light is turning golden
as the sun sinks today,
and I want to go back.
Even if I should die,
if I was on my journey, well—
the earth is a mother who always
claims her lost children.

When the world comes to an end
Tap pa akuē apāxāi tukuēt

Our stories and our songs told us
of the beginning of the world,
the gushing of creation from the sacred springs,
the beginning of fire, of stars and lightning,
the sun and moon, and the four colors.
The reason for rain, and the good herbs,
and the thorn trees. How deer and coyote
and possum came to be, and how
the first people sprang up from
the earth and increased.

There was no end time in our stories,
or in our songs, which had passed
from grandparent to grandchild,
since the beginning.

Now the priests tell us
the world will end.
This we believe.
Is it not already ending?
Where are the many grandchildren
who will remember our stories?
Who will remember how to speak
our words, how to sing our songs,
who will remember our names?
Where are the grandparents to teach this?
They fall and disappear like drops
of rain on thirsty ground.

When the world comes to an end,
tap pa akuē apāxāi tukuēt,
then the people who were good,

the priests tell us,
will live again.

Perhaps—we may help the world end.
Now when we dance, at night, and in secret,
where we once danced in thanks for rain,
or a good war, or a good hunt,
now we dance to bring
the end of the world.
When the world comes to an end,
tap pa akuē apāxāi tukuēt,
the good people will live again.

We sing—
Let it come! Hey! Let it end!
Let the good people live again!
When the world comes to an end!

This is going to come to pass
Ampakāl san apām

I once told the people what I dreamt,
but I was only a boy.
I had never before taken
our sacred cactus drink.

But I knew what I dreamt.

I drank, and I fell down,
and when I stood again,
my feet took root.
As fast as my roots plunged down,
my body grew up, shooting
to the sky like the lanky sunflower.
Higher and higher I grew,
until, swaying, I could see
past the river, past the burning plains,
and into the far mountains of the south.

And from the mountains,
I saw a small dot fly out.
The dot grew bigger and bigger,
the way a dark swarm of insects
grows in view. But the dot
was a shadow, and the shadow
began to eat the land,
the way shadow is said
to eat the sun, every tenth generation.
The people danced, and prayed,
and sang, but they could not
send the shadow back.

I told them this was what I dreamt.
This is going to come to pass!
Ampakāl san apām!
My people only laughed.
And I myself could not know fully
what it meant.

But now, an old man, I have seen
the shadow of pestilence,
the shadow of slavery,
the shadow of sadness, and
great griefs, *apat'akāl' apnākan*.

Now, an old man, I no longer need
the cactus, so easy do I pass
into dreams and daytime sleep.
I hobble no farther than the field
and church, yet in my dreams,
I see the shadow sweeping on
to lands unknown to me, to red deserts,
to great plains and mountains.
I see unknown women and children,
slain or weeping in snow.

I tell no one now, but I know—
Ampakāl san apām!
This is going to come to pass!

II.

nāko
to think

xt'ēwal
to anger

tālam
to fear

In this world
Tap pa akuēt

In this world, *tap pa akuēt*,
nearly everything is bad, or so
the priests tell us. The sacred color
we use to mark the bodies of our youth,
the medicine from cactus thumbs
and beans of mountain laurel,
the couplings of man and woman.

What do the priests know about this world?
I think they know no more
than the dark and solitary spider
who builds the ground trap, covering it
with the frill of green lichen, springing
out to seize his meat. The spider
knows only his earthen hole, and
the small world around its door.

I, an old woman, who can walk only
half a day, still know more about this world than they do.
Where to find the good roots when their purple flowers
are gone in winter, where to find the fat grubs
and the small ground bees, which earth
is best to mix with our pounded beans
and which best to make our sacred paints,
when to burn the placenta to spare
the stillborn's spirit, where and when is best
to make a baby who will be a son.

Tap pa akuīkuēx, here in this world,
everything is bad, they say.
Even the priests' god left this world.
He had a chance to live again, but—

uxuāl' tukuēt apamāo saux apām,
he ascended into heaven.

Live well, they tell me, and you too
might leave this world.

But if the priests know so little in this world,
how can they tell us with certainty
that the next world will be so good?

Have you made fun of them?
Mamīkaxāmayasauxuam ē?

Nooooo, I said, in answer to the priests.
That was not what I was doing,
when I made to pick up
invisible skirts, laughing and stumbling.
No, I would not make fun
of the bald clumsy men,
the men who would stumble
in their grey rags and beads
if I decided to stomp and leap away.

Do they think to trap me
with a douse of water on the head?

They fish with a hole in their net;
theirs bows are not strung.

Do they think I am as foolish as a deer
who comes every day the same time
and place to water?

Ho! Hey!

I may eat their food,
I may come when I need,
but I will go
when I want.

Like the deer
who returns to the mountain.

Twice twenty and ten
Taiwakō axtē ko xūyopamāux axtē

Thus our people count.

Twenty
Taiwakō

Twenty and one
Taiwakō ko pil'

Twenty and ten
Taiwakō ko xūyopamāux axtē

Twice twenty
Taiwakō axtē

Twice twenty and ten
Taiwakō axtē ko xūyopamāux axtē

The priests laugh at our way of counting.
But it is easy for them to count one by one.
All that they count stands still—
their bits of silver, their candles,
their bags of seed and wool.

But anyway, we knew
they would not know counting,
once they told us of their god.

Father, son, and spirit.

How many gods are there?
T'āxat Dios apsā tcē osā ē ?

They ask us again,
T'āxat Dios apsā tcē osā ē ?
How many gods are there?

Axtikpīl'.
Three.
Of course.

My soul
Napāxam

To the mission, we came in surrender,
clutching the hands of our last children.

Is it not enough that now we put our hands
to the plow and the loom, that with our hands
we take up strange tools
to tear the earth to get our food,
that we have put on the rough garments?
Is it not enough that we have taken root
around the mission like seedlings
around a tree, no longer free
like wind and birds?

No, it is not enough. The priests
want more from the people. They want
their souls, *apaxam apsā*.

The priests besiege us with words.
Nākak'tāi! I entreat you!
Tzin nakaxuākam! I beg you!

But my soul has taken cover
deep inside me, and I watch
their words spill in front of me
the way rain spills across the mouth
of a sheltering riverbank cave.
They do not touch me.

I will give the priests
my hands, *namāux*.

But I will not give them
my soul, *napaxām*.

Words
Pilāpaxlē

As a youth I was enslaved to serve
in a household to the south.
Returned with the priests to the land
of my birth and my people,
now I serve them both,
or so I tell myself.

I am a cord pulled tautly between them,
or so it feels. With the priests
I teach Spanish to the people. From the people
I gather words and teach them to the priests,
which they mark down on paper.
My days are filled with talking and talking,
and the scratching sound of the priests' quills.

I never went on the hunt, but I remember
seeing our men drive animals into a narrow gully,
and I remember how I held my breath,
wondering which would pass through alive.
So it is with words, *pilāpaxlē*.
Which will come out alive?

Some of the words I try to teach the priests,
they do not care to catch and mark:
the age of the deer with her spotted coat,
the autumn clouds like scales of a fish,
or the bush with thorns like claws of a cat,
of which there is no other like it.

Instead, we must talk and talk
about more swift and darting prey,
what we believe, or feel, what we know,

or places and beings not seen or known.
Here I walk so carefully along the cord,
back and forth, carrying these words.

But I know sometimes I fail, I fall.
How will the priests write down
what we know as *xuāi* ,
how can I tell them all that we know
of the places where we exist?
The word will become only—
mission, village, house, or town.

And the truth—*pimān pax*—
How do we know truth, we the people?
From the voice and face and body
of the one who speaks it, or conceals it,
or from the good or ill it brings.
For the priests, truth is in the book
they show when they preach,
the book that holds *apaxlē tutcēn*,
the things God has spoken,
fixed for all time.

The people sometimes ask me—
did the god make this book with his own hand?
I explain to them that, no, it was told to ones
like me and to the priests, who caught the words,
understood them, and marked them down.
But to myself I wonder: what if those
who caught and fixed the words of God,
were not so careful as I am?

Naxopimāma
Our Father

The priests speak of their god—
Naxopimāma pō, he is our father.

But there is no father like that.
I do not believe.

Xak'makōxsāux!
Kneel down!

The priests make me gaze
at the god's poor son,
his bloodless and naked body,
the dart wound in his side,
twisted on his wooden tree,
with thorns on his head.

There is no father
who would give his son to such torture,
there is no father who could look down,
day after day, to watch such torture.

For what reason?
The son was good, the priests say.
He was healthy. He was a man.
He was not born a twin,
or a misshapen body, or an extra girl.
And of all those who must die,
none of us would wish
to watch them suffer.

Xak'makōxsāux!
Kneel down!

As a boy, when I first saw a mouse pinned
to the spike of the yucca by the crafty shrike,
when I first saw the small rabbit pierced
by my trap of the lotebush thorns,
their eyes were half-closed,
like those of the son on his tree.
And I, even a boy, took pity
on those poor beings.

The priests speak of their god—
Naxopimāma pō,
He is our father.
But this I do not believe.
There is no father
who would mock his son such a way,
day after day, dying forever.

He will cast them into hell
T'oaxām tukuēt akpahākoxt'ām sanpō

In my waking hours, I have almost forgotten,
in so short a time, what it was like
to run alongside the men, my father, my uncles,
following the animals we hunted.

In my dreaming, I am there again.
I am in the hunt. But in my dreaming,
I am the hunted. I am the deer
running and running and running,
and stumbling. I wake panting.

I am the deer running
and leaping. I am the deer,
knowing my breast
will be pierced with the arrow.
Or I am the peccary,
flailing and falling
through the dead leaves
into the cunning trap, knowing
the darts will rain down.
And I wake screaming.

Or I am myself, but I am running
and running from the wall
of prairie flame that is surging
in front of the shouting men
with our bows and arrows.
I wake shouting.

Now the priests begin to ask me
if I am bewitched. Is there
a woman or man, a witch or wizard,
who troubles my dreams?

Do they not see
that their own god has done it?

Do they not tell me, always, a sinner—
T'oaxām tukuēt akpahākoxt'ām sanpō!
He will cast them into hell!

Do they not tell me that in hell,
piltcē watzamōxuaxāmatē, pilāpaxuāx sāux tcoxāi
there is no sleeping, there is no resting.

Every night in my dreams,
I am running, but the flames
of hell come closer.

I am worth nothing
Pīntci nakāmmam axām

No matter what we suffered,
I knew my worth. I knew
because I yet remembered
the parents who traded us, my sister and I,
to the Spaniard and his wife.
My father had held my hand.
And then, his hand held the reins
of the dappled horses he led away,
with woollen blankets on their back,
and sacks of corn. My mother had
carried my smaller sister. And then, her arms
held cloth, a cloak, a bag of food,
a bag of beads, a silver bracelet.

I remembered their backs, their arms,
as they walked away, heavy with our worth
which would feed and clothe many.

I knew our worth, traded for our bodies,
and for our work. No matter what we suffered,
always, I remembered our worth.

But then, my sister died.
I will not say how. Soon after,
the priest came and brought me
to the mission. Had he bought me?

I think not.
Although the priest saved me,
he also taught me—

Pīntci nakāmmam axām,
I am worth nothing.
So we say in the confession.

It is my sins that count for something.
It is sin that I carry. I can only work,
and pray. I pray for God
to take away my heavy sins,
to make me worthy someday
to fly to heaven. Even though—
pīntci nakāmmam axām,
I am worth nothing.

Witch
Yēwal

Tshhh, tshhh, my mother says,
and lays her hand on me.
But I'm still afraid of the hooting birds
I hear sometimes at night.
I'm afraid of the tangled trees
just past the mission fields
where my father works each day.

But I'm most afraid
of the ugly painted woman
who lives among us.
She is so old, I am sure
she is a witch! *Yēwal!*

Her face is another tangle,
of strange, painted lines and spots,
mixed up with wrinkles.

I'm afraid when she tries
to touch my face or hair
with her patchy hands and ragged nails.
I'm afraid of what poison
may be inside the pouch of rabbit skin
she carries within her skirt.
I have heard she leaves the mission
when the moon is dark.

Once, when I was sick, she tried
to place strange powders in my food.
Twice, I have dropped my skein of thread
when she walked by, and once
I stumbled hard when she looked at me!

I do not care that she is
the mother of my father,
I call her—
Yēwal! Witch!

III.

hōi
to make, to do, to commit
to become
to work

malkūita
to confess
(possibly from Spanish, *mal cuidar*)

tānko
to command
to order

What is your name?
T'āhaka xaxauxuē ?

That was my first and greatest mistake,
to answer them.
T'āhaka xaxauxuē ?
What is your name?

Taxum !
Tell me!
Tzin naktānko .
I command you.

I was tired and my stomach empty,
and there seemed no harm
in telling my name to someone
too stupid to know it is rude to ask,
who could only say a few words
in the language of the people.

But from then on, there has been no escape
from the loud reach of my name
in the mouths of the grey-clothed priests.
Even when I am in the farthest field,
or beyond the sound of the clanging bells,
hunting in what was once my home,
I feel their windy breath on me,
saying my name in their clumsy way.

Once, my name was good.
Now it's only good the way a single
chili tree is good, shining with its red
fruit in the dense woods—
good to draw the grey singing birds
to devour its goodness.

Now the priests command me
twice twenty and ten times a day,
and my name is always at the beginning of—
do this, do that, like the tip
of the ax that begins the work
of breaking the wood.
Do this, do that.
Tzin naktānko,
I command you.

Have you danced the mitote?
Txē mamaixā yam ē?

When they ask us this,
I believe the priests are afraid.
Have you danced the mitote?
Txē mamaixā yam ē ?
Did you become intoxicated?
Mamāiyāman am ē ?

They know the answer.
They know we slip away at night,
walk quietly the path in the woods
to a clearing, to a warm fire within
the streaming circle of dancers.

We joy in the clacking sticks of ebony,
the rattle of pebbles within the gourds,
the deep-chested voice of the taut drum,
and the rumble of our many feet moving.
With the *samīn,* with the *paxē*—
with the red seeds of mountain laurel
and the cactus thumbs—
we worship. We worship our gods
with our bodies, our feet, and our voices—
and they answer us! With the voice
of the owl, with the voice of the nighthawk,
and with our dreams, they answer.
Our gods are alive and moving with us.

Have you danced the mitote?
Txē mamaixā yam ē?
Did you become intoxicated?
Mamāiyāman am ē?

Yes, we dance, and drink,
drum, and dream,
and the priests fear it.
They make us confess to it
before we pray, before we kneel
in the cold church where our knees ache.
There, their painted god and holy ones
look down on us, without speech,
without movement or breath. For this,
I believe the priests are afraid
of our living gods.

They do not know, and we do not tell them,
that sometimes when we dance and dream,
even their god, the little child, *t'anpam can,*
he also speaks to us!

Mamāyayūnayām ē ?
Did you fast?

Until the priests taught us,
we had not known that going
without food made us holy.

How holy were we, then,
in the long months of hunger,
when the animals hid all day in the deep thickets?
How holy, after the good mesquite beans
had all been pounded, and their dried flatcakes eaten,
or in the still-cold month when the roots
sprouted and turned bitter?

We thought we were most holy
when with joy we sometimes shared
the roasted meat of a deer with our people,
and the wives carried their savory portion
to our parents. We thought we were holy
when we laughed from the sweet juice
of the cactus tuna dripping down the childrens' chins,
and there was more fruit than our bellies could hold.
We thought such feasts holy.

But now we know—
we were only full of food,
not spirit.

The priests ask me,
Mamāyayūnayām ē ?
Did you fast?

Now I am only a lonely widower
who is glad of a meal each morning

at the mission, but still I wonder
over the trade we have made.

It is true that fewer days now
my stomach clings to my spine.
A few hours or days of fasting
means nothing to me.
But the small pieces of bread, *ax xuīzkuan,*
for which we sometimes fast—
they do not fill me
the way the wild feasts did.

Do not be ashamed before me
Tiaxuānkam axām kām

Tell me all your sins, the priest says.
Do not be ashamed before me,
tiaxuānkam axām kām.

I can give him a few confessions.
It is easy to remember some small untruth,
some morning I slept past the ringing of the bell.
And, I dance the mitote, it is true, and that
I can confess, a gift to the priest
to receive my penance in return.

But it seems I can't give answers
good enough
to so many of his questions.
Questions that he asks as though
he has heard stories.

He asks me about
unchaste things,
pinwak xuanīkahamē apsakām.
What can I tell him?
My woman and I are satisfied
with each other. I was never
clever enough to think of all
these other people, parts, and places
he asks about, that might have been
vessels for my lust.

He asks me about anger,
he asks me about stealing.
And what can I tell him?
I am satisfied with my bow,

my quiver, my tools,
and need no one else's.
I am satisfied with my people,
and slow to anger.

The worse the sin, the more
eagerly he asks.
He asks me about killing, as if
he has heard stories.

Mamaitcāp am ē?
Did you kill someone?

T'āxat apsakām mamiktcāpko yam ē?
How many did you kill?

It is true sometimes we went to war
and killed and were killed. But me?
I can't claim such deeds.
What can I tell him?
Often when we went to war,
we shouted, and our women shouted and sang,
and we shot our arrows above
the tops of the huisache and mesquite,
until the enemy waded back across
the creek, or fled into the forest.

If the priest asked these questions
in anger, I might be tempted to lie
and boast of many sins.

But, no, he asks with the coaxing voice
of a child who is hungry
for another piece of meat.

He says,

Do not be ashamed before me.
Tiaxuānkam axām kām.

I cannot lie to such a voice.
But I am beginning to be ashamed
that I am not the man
he thinks I am!

For how many years have you been sinning with this woman?
T'āxat āxakō aptcīka tāgu pitapōyō saxpām pinapsā mahōi salatē?

I laughed at the priest's question.
Years enough!
Enough years that five times my wife
took to the woods with her womenfolk
to bare our children, and five times
I reclined on the hides to receive
the hearty slaps and cheers of our men.
And of these five, two children lived,
and now reach the time
to make children of their own.

What rites do she and I need further?
When I first took the good deer meat
and the two turkeys with the fine feathers
to her family, I was invited to eat.

Since then, we have danced with
the people, and we have sung.
We have shared food and famine together.

The only rite left for her
will be to cry and pluck her hair
when someday I die.

Have you lived in concubinage with any man?
Xak'āu mām ē?

How should I answer this?
Since the day of his gifts to my family,
I have lived with this man.
For him I made smooth the deerskins,
for him I gathered the sweetest fruit.
With him I bore five children,
two now grown to youth.
When he went to war,
with my own trembling fingers
I put the paint on his face,
solemn as mine. When he left
I cried encouragement and shouts,
and when he returned,
I cried in gladness.

So, whatever rite is necessary I will make,
that we may stay together, always,
in this life and the next.

Have you been angry with some man?
Mamayāxt'ēgulo yam ē?

Matzān, younger brother
born to our mother and father,
I will not tell in the confession
about the war between us,
the argument that divided us
and split one family from another,
as the people quarreled
over what was wisdom
and what was fear.

Oh my brother,
I remember when years ago you first began
to overtake me, a sapling grown to tree.
You outstripped me in our races across the short grass,
and our playful wrestling turned to brawls.
It was you who always brought down
the finest deer, with your bow of anacua.
You became as hard as its wood,
and as taut as its bowstring,
never slack, and never failing.

Of course you would lead
the party of war, and you would take
the angry young men to the woods
to live the old ways, to make raids
and sallies against these strangers.

And now they ask me in confession,
Have you been angry with some man?
Mamayāxt'ēgulo yam ē?

Xakuātzum ē?
Did you pardon this man?

Oh my brother,
in two languages I pray for you.
You called us rabbits who came
here to the mission, fleeing to warrens.
You believed you carried within you
the courage of the wolf
who fiercely defends its forest.
But, *matzān,* younger brother,
may you also be wary as the spotted cat
at twilight, and fleet as the pronghorn.
May wind and rain erase your tracks,
and before we die, may we
both learn to pardon, as easily
as morning pardons night.

How many people are there?
T'āxat apsākapā?

The slow one, the dull one,
the laggard. That is what I was,
before the mission.

When I came here,
I was glad of the new name,
Pedro, and the new work.
And when the priests gave me keys,
they said I would be like my namesake,
trusted with the keys to heaven.

I became the quick one,
the clever one, the one close
at hand. I learned to always
walk nearby the priests.
I learned the names of the strange things
and strange animals of the mission.
And I learned their numbers
to a hundred, and more.

There was no limit to my counting.
I could go very far, always walking
at the right hand of the priest
who wrote and asked,
Xat? How many?

Missals, chalices, censers, cruets,
chasubles, surplices,
capes and cloaks.

Xat? How many?
Ribbons, pins, fringes, lace,

cards, combs, and shuttles,
boxes, cabinets, and crates.

Xat? How many?
Chisels and yokes and hoes,
shovels and shears, kettles, jugs,
skimmers, skillets, dippers.

Xat? How many?
Jennies and jacks,
mares, stallions, and colts,
ewes and rams and lambs.

And some days—
T'āxat apsākapā?
How many people are there?

And then, I would count the baptized
and the catechumens,
the men with women and children,
the widows and widowers,
the bachelors, and the orphans.

One day, the numbers
were not right. I counted again.
The priest asked again,
T'āxat apsākapā?
How many people are there?

The numbers were not right.
From this, the priests saw
that five had fled.
From this, the soldiers went
to bring them back.
From this, the people learned
the word for fugitive.

From this, the fugitives learned
the strength of fetters and of stocks.
From this, I learned
the fearsome power of counting.

God commands
Dios po watānko

I was one who helped the priests
build the mission church.
The heavy blocks were brought by oxcart,
and with sweat and toil made into walls
that rose higher than trees.
I had no fear of climbing,
and so I set the highest blocks.
Looking down from high above, I paused,
and saw what god must see.
I saw how it must be when
dios po watānko, god commands.

Among our people, no one had commanded.
We had followed, above all, the seasons,
going where and when the cactus fruit ripened,
the mesquite beans sweetened, the deer fattened.
And when the people could not agree,
our dreams guided us, or we used
our songs and stories to stir others,
the way the wind blows low across
the prairie, and stirs the tall grass.

But, now, from far above, in heaven,
dios po watānko, god commands.
And below him, the priests tell us,
there is a man, a king, who also sits
high above the people on a fine seat,
and who commands his men,
who have yet other men. And here,
there are the soldiers, and the settlers,
and the priests, though they cannot agree
who among them should command us.

Even the people now command.
The priests teach us to command the animals
which way to go, so that we may
ride them or herd them or milk them,
mark them as belonging to the mission.
We command the plants where to grow
and when and how, with our hoes and plows.
We command the earth itself, with ditches
that tell the water where to flow.

And all this I saw and understood
when I helped set the heavy blocks
upon the wall. From on high,
dios po watānko, god commands,
and the weight of his commands
the world bears from below.

IV.

xāmtzam
to wish
to desire

tzakēx
to seek someone
to visit

saayēx
to need
to be lacking

mi
to own
to possess

He has come to visit you
Mamāk kamām tcon

The priests watch us, the girls,
when the young men come to the mission.
The priests smile and tend us
like the tuberose they grow
to place upon the altars.

But I know the same priests use us
like a lure for men outside the mission,
as the tuberose brings the fathers' honeybees.

Nak'āi axām, let him not touch.
Cover yourself, they tell us.
Cast down your eyes.

Let other girls be soft and falling
as a petal. I am a hunter.
I have my eyes on one,
the one with a crooked smile.

Mamāk kamām tcon,
he has come to visit you,
they tell me. I know.
He circles like a bird over water
because I call to him. I am a hunter.
I hunt him in stillness and quiet, and
I make a call. I call to him in the old songs,
and I hum our old songs as I walk.

Mamāk kamām tcon,
He has come to visit you.

It is autumn now, and he circles
like the arriving geese.
But I will bring him in by winter.
I want him beside me in the winter,
warm, with a fire
and four thick walls around us.

And there, I will throw the first cord around him—
of love. The priests will make him marry me.
They will ask him,
Mamāik'āi am ē?
Have you touched?

But he will barely resist.
By then I will be making the second cord—
a child I will bear before next year's geese arrive.
We will baptize our child, and we will both
lay down our hunting bows.

She was shut in
Apot'āwaxōpē

Pray to the holy virgin mother,
the priests tell us,
that she will be your friend.

They tell us of her wondrous life.
Like a young girl, her womb was always closed.
She was shut in, *apot'āwaxōpē*.

Yet she bore a son,
and when she bore him, she had no pain.
She did not lose blood, *ahātz tā apahōux sal axām*.

She lost her son to death,
and yet, a god,
he returned to life!
Apatpāyamtzanām apām!

Could such a strange mother
have pity on me, a common woman?
I want only one human son to live.
My womb is not shut in.
I gladly bear my children in blood and pain.
But which of these has survived?
The boy born before his time.
The boy born with the clouded eyes,
and the nose from which water flowed.
The girl who withered and died
in her first month, smaller than
when she left my womb.

I desire only one son
to live his given years.

My husband and I despair
and grow angry with each other.
But we are not allowed to find
new spouses to give us living children.
As surely as if they tied our hands
with a thong of strong hide,
the priests bind us to each other,
and to a future of dead children.

I look at the calm face of the holy virgin mother.
Her womb was shut in, *apot'āwaxōpē*.
She knew no men.
For that, I call her blessed!

Those who wish to marry
Ax xek'ātzawamkē tapamō axpam

Those who wish to marry
must be patient as snails,
and unmoved as stones,
while the priests ask their questions
to find out who is who
and who will be allowed
to marry.

Is he married?
Apatayagu pō ē?
Are you single?
Pil' mameyatāgū yaxām ē?

Is he your elder brother?
Xaxat'al po ē?
Is she your younger sister?
Xayat'ān po ē?
Is he your nephew?
Xakant'ān po ē?
Is she your stepmother?
Xatapāi po ē?

I was not patient with such questions.
A year ago a son of my people
desired to marry me. But—
it was early fall, the freshening winds
were stirring me. I shook seed heads
ferociously to scatter them, felt myself float
among the fire-colored butterflies
streaming south above the mission.

I was not unmoved.
While the priests went on with their questions,
to needlessly untangle who was who,
I rode away with a smiling muleteer
who was passing through.

Do you really desire to marry?
Mak xanayē xamīn pil' mameyak'āu atāpamo kalō yam ē ?

I have always been a favorite
of the priests and the people.
Not because I was left an orphan
in care of all. Not because
my slender tongue took to both languages.
Not because my swift fingers sewed
a seam or twirled a spindle quick and neat.
Not even because my swift mind learned
the answers to the catechism.

I know it is because
my eyes are black and big as a doe's,
and my hair shines like a falcon's wing.
Many hands have been laid
in gentleness or envy
atop my shining hair!

Now they ask—
Do you really desire to marry?
Mak xanayē xamīn pil' mameyak'āu atāpamo kalō yam ē ?

The priests and the people—
He is a soldier, the priests say.
He is Spanish, the people say.

Do you really desire to marry?
Mak xanayē xamīn pil' mameyak'āu atāpamo kalō yam ē ?

But my doe eyes see what life will be.
Does it matter which man owns
the loom where I sit? This one, too,

will lay his heavy hand atop my head.
He, too, will feed me morsels
from white plates with swirling blue bands.
And the priests have promised me
a silver thimble at my marriage.

Did you steal anything?
Pin pil' mā xōuxtcā'akē xō ē?

At first we did not understand
when the priests asked us this.
Why would we steal? Only children
have not learned to share.

The priests say they give us
the light of the world, but to me,
everything at this place
is half-lit, shadowed.

Before, we were either hungry, or fed.
It was night or it was day.
We were alive, or we were dead.
At times, we wanted, but we knew
what it was we wanted—
some food, drink, sleep or dreams,
running or rest, a mate or a child.
Everything was in its season,
and one had only to wait.

Nōuxtcālak axām, I do not steal.
I am not a child who has not learned to share.
Would I, a granny, steal?
Have I held back my food from children
and children's children? Have I not shared
my sharpest digging sticks and bone needles
with sisters and wives of brothers?
Are not my pendants of mussel shells
among the finest, and have I not
given them to anyone
who has looked at them with pleasure?
There was a river-full of shells,

and a season in which to shape them.
And if in anything I wanted, I also
was given, if it was possible.

Nōuxtcālak axām, I do not steal.
And how could I?
There is plenty enough, more,
brought with each long line of oxen or mules,
things bright or dull, soft or sharp,
food and tools, glittering things,
scented things for the church.
And all these things the priests
take out from the hide or wooden trunks,
and put away, with lock upon lock—
we had not known locks—
where we cannot touch, look,
pass from hand to hand, use.
One day a priest took me by the wrist,
dragged me to kneel in front of the weeping mother
who looks out from the church wall.
Pin t'āxat apsakām xōuxtcālakē?
What thing did you steal?
And again he asks me,
Pin t'āxat apsakām xōuxtcālakē?

Yes! I stole. The sky-blue covering
that they put on the mother's head,
I took it, and put it underneath
the corn shucks that I sleep on.
Why? I do not know.
I took it, but there was no
pleasure in having it.

Now I must make penance.
In the half-light of the church,
with its flickering smoky candles,

I rub my eyes and I look at the mother,
and at her son, and her husband
with his staff. I am supposed to get something
from them, but I do not know what.
Life after death? What does that mean?
And what good is that when, here,
life itself is locked away?

I am very much pleased
Tzin nikāwa sāux pam

My child will thrive.
I will do all I can for her,
even as my husband
each day falls away from us.

With only half a heart,
he sets off slowly in the morning
for the fields, and returns slowly
at the call of the bell. Perhaps
his soul has been stolen,
or wandered off to the woods.
He is so silent.

I am sorry for him,
but then I see my small girl
and hear her happy twitter.
So I am quick to the call of the bell.
I am the first to say the prayers,
the first to sweep in the morning,
the last to put away my spindle.

When he counts my skeins of yarn,
the priest tells me,
Tzin nikāwa sāux pam,
I am very much pleased.

When he sees my pretty daughter
wind the wool, or lisp her prayer,
or with her plump hand make
a clumsy sign of the cross,
the priest gives her a ribbon.

Axōminō, he says—
because you are very good.

Of all the women, only I have
an extra petticoat. Only we receive
an extra chili in our basket,
an extra handkerchief.
Even for my husband,
I get tobacco, and our blanket
is the heaviest and the best
among the people.

For this—
tzin nikāwa sāux pam,
I am very much pleased.

All the things the priests have taught me
Kutātze tupā takpaxātzo wakō tutcēn

I will make good use of those things
when I leave here. The bargain was fair.

I was hungry, and they fed me.
I was naked, and they clothed me.
They gave me *xō*, understanding,
and new tools and a new language.
And for them I broke their fields,
built their church, and answered
to their bell. I knelt, I prayed,
I confessed my most secret sins.

But now I am tired of the bell,
I am tired of every day—the same.
I remember too well how pleasant
it is to walk where I want, or to sleep
if I want, in the sun on a cool afternoon.
I am tired of answering to the priests,
and their many commands,
and their many questions.

Bezerro tapā pil'amīka mē ?
This calf, who does it belong to?
Pin t'āxat apsakām xōuxtcālakē?
What thing did you steal?
Mamaiāx tzanām am ē?
Did you give it back?

I will not give it back.
I have given enough. Indeed,
I will take the calf, and the clothes I wear.

I will take a blanket, some seed, and perhaps—
take the girl with the dimpled smile.

I will take the words I learned,
and their god, now my god, *Dios namī*.
I will leave and not come back,
and when I leave, I will even take
Santo Angel tapkuām tupōyō,
the holy angel that takes care of me.

The priests told me that inside one soul—
Pīnta apaxō sāux pa usā, there is understanding;
and I have it.
Pīnta apaxām sāux pa usā, there is memory;
and I keep it.
Co pīnta apakawa sāux pa usā, and there is will;
and I use it.

V.

mestīa
to pray
(possibly from Spanish, *menester*)

kuām
to hope
to wait for

spāmo
to believe

kāwa
to love
to be joyful

We will speak to God
Dios tupōm niyolātze wakō kam

O god bright as the sun,
warm as the fire,
see us, your people,
gathered here among the strangers.
Gathered in fear of our enemies.
Gathered in fear of hunger, and of pestilence.
We are like the speckled pink doves
who sleep piled atop each other in the trees,
huddled against the cold—
and this is our winter.

O god bright as the sun,
send an end to our winter,
that we may fly out again across the land,
live in the dappled shade of the mesquite,
build our shelter from limbs and grass,
gather our food from the good earth,
and give birth to our young.

O god bright as the sun,
see your people gathered here!
Send an end to our winter
that we may fly away!

Are you a witch?
Xapakuāxo ē?

I became as still as a fawn in the grass.

The priest asked again,
Are you a witch?
Xapakuāxo ē?

I became as quiet as a rabbit.

My mouth would not shape an answer.
Would I be blamed for a stillbirth,
an accident with a wayward adze,
or an illness among the children?

But it was help, not blame, the priest hunted!
A nearby soldier was bewitched
and could not get well. We went.
With feathery stems of silver wormwood
and with my stroking touch,
I helped him expel a clot of deadly phlegm.
But I also saw the hope in the sick man's gaze
when the priest prayed and raised
their god's cross above him.
Such hope that it seemed like fire
flickered through his ashen face.

I always knew that each plant,
each object, had its virtue.
At that moment, with the deep sight
we sometimes gained with our dance and drink,
I knew that god was everywhere the same,
and through god, all good grew.

The priest explained—
Pīnwak apahōi apām,
He does all things.

Praise to god and his son
I sing the loudest now,
and the priests allow me
to love god
by healing his people.

I hope
Nakuām

I think the priests are not subtle.
They see only two ways.
They keep only two lists.
What we must do—
work, pray, fast, confess, believe, hope—
and what we must not do—
idle, steal, lie, fornicate, flee,
dance, drink, gamble.

But in life, day shades into night,
and night fades into day.

Did I hope, or did I gamble,
when I came here to the mission?
It was not a game, that is true.
My son had died in sweat and filth,
and my good wife was sick.
I hoped that the strangers who
brought pestilence to the people
might also know how to cure it.

I hoped the priests would cure her,
when they took my wife,
cleaned her, laid her down,
sang strange words over her,
and rubbed a grease upon her
forehead, breast, hands, and feet.
I hoped, but she died just the same.
My good wife died!

I could have left the mission.
But the priests told me

their god Jesus Christ will raise the dead.
He will make them return to life,
akpatpāyokām wakō tzanam in sanpō.
He raises them, *wakcōtē.*

And so, I stayed.
I work, pray, fast, confess, believe,
and I hope, *nakuām.*
Or, do I gamble?
On this one tale they told—
that He raises them, w*atcōnō.*

I know this—I am wagering
all that is left to me,
all that is left of me,
that this one tale be true.

God will pardon you
Dios tupō makpakuātzum san tupāyō

I will not forget the day the priests taught me—
Dios tupō makpakuātzum san tupāyō,
God will pardon you!

They told me—
Speak to him, *xaxlē wakōx!*
Say with me, *tāxanē xaxlē,*
the prayers to him.
And from that moment
I learned the power of words
was better than dreams or dance.
In my language I poured out
the heavy sickness I had carried—

When the rains stayed away,
the beans shriveled on the trees,
the deer were gaunt,
and the doe lost her fawns,
then the mothers of the people
had also to lose their babies.
Better to die quickly and be covered
by the smothering loam,
than to live and starve.

But when it was my own baby!
With her last cry, a heavy weight
entered me and took her place,
so that those around me thought
I was bewitched.

My grief was great, heavier than
the heaviest wood I carried on my back.

My step was slow and burdened.
I could not dance or sing.
No one and no medicine
could comfort me, or stop my weeping.

From the priests I learned
the source of sickness. It was—
my sins, *pin napsak'āux!*
Now, my back is still burdened
with bundles of wood, and my arms
are now weighted with the broom,
and the work of the loom and the spindle.
But such heaviness spills and leaves me
when daily I say my prayers and remember
the words the priests taught—
Dios tupō makpakuātzum san tupāyō!
God will pardon you!

I believe it
Naspāmo

I believe in the new way.
The young men scorn me
that I, an elder, give up
the old ways.

But I have seen enough to know
the way of life is change.
I have seen when a great storm
makes the river jump its bank
and carve a new course.
Do we try to make the river
run in its old course?

I believe in the new way,
which is both hard and easy.
The priests mark the way
for us as plainly as a trodden
path in the forest. They tell us
what we must do, and not do,
what we must believe,
and not believe, and
I believe it, *naspāmo*.

If the doing and not doing
are sometimes hard,
I remember that it was also hard
to be the good hunter that I was.

I remember the many hours I spent
chipping the finest points, the hours
of straightening shafts of arrows

along the narrow and hard
grooves of a stone.

I remember the way my eyes
found the only path an arrow must take
to reach the animal that became
the next day's feast.

So, too, the priests tell us
that this new way
is a hard and narrow path,
that leads to a good place.
I believe it, *naspāmo*.

I will hone myself against the stone
of the new way, and when I die,
I will fly straight and true
to the new heaven in the sky.

Because you love me much
Taxakāwa pam inō

The older of the priests
would tell me this, smiling,
whenever I brought his staff,
helped him with the animals,
opened the heavy log gates.
It was a joke I thought, the way
he joked of being one we called
xat'al, elder brother of a man,
elder brother to me.

No. I might do this or that for him,
but it was not for love.
Only pity for this aging man.
Knowing that a few years
would bring me to this, also.

Taxakāwa pam inō.
Because you love me much.

No. I might help him, and hear him,
but I did not listen to his talk
of new life, love, of brothers
and brotherhood, of a father above us,
whom we must love and pray to.

Taxakāwa pam inō.
Because you love me much.

No. When I was not working,
my mind still roamed the forest,
lived the time when I could leap
as well as the deer I chased,

when I shouted with my brothers of the hunt,
when we marked ourselves
with the blood of deer and peccary,
danced in our wild celebrations,
in our wild freedom.
Where were those brothers now?
Fled, or dead.

Then one night the elder priest called me
I dare to ask from my half-sleep—
What do you want? Why do you want me?

Taxakāwa pam inō,
because you love me much,
he laughed, and shoved a taper at me to carry.
I followed him to a pen where
one of the female animals labored.
We knelt shoulder to shoulder
within the small circle of light.
I watched this strange man
reach inside the straining animal,
and bring out the life inside her.
He wiped away the slime and blood,
pressed air into the small creature's lungs
and pushed it to its mother.
He and I laughed and slapped each other
on the shoulders, as the animal arched its back
against the licking of the mother's rough tongue.

Now I remember this time, as often
as I think of the wild hunts.

At night, after working with the young men,
and the animals, shepherding them both,
and after evening prayers,
I visit my brother, and when I bow,

he greets me—Here you are,
taxakāwa pam inō.
because you love me much.

Be joyful!
Xikāwa sāux!

I believe it, *naspāmo*—
our lord's resurrection—
because I, too, have risen from the dead.

When we came to the mission, I died
an ugly death, like a fish that curls
and flops for a long time on land,
unable to breathe or swim
outside its natural waters.

And then I slowly came to life again,
learned to move and breathe.
I learned the feel of walls around me,
I learned the yoke and plow.
I learned to kneel and pray.

And now, if anyone listens to an old man
with a strange language, I tell them,
Xikāwa sāux, be joyful!

Be joyful that the virgin mother of god
weeps with us over the children lost,
and rejoices with us over living children.
Be joyful with each child born
who has the eyes of our people,
and the color of our people.

Be joyful that the saints, the friends of god,
Ysidro, Antonio, José, and Juan,
hear our prayers and help us,
and that the flute of war now warbles

in tune with our voices,
praising the true god.

Be joyful, too, that our cousin
the coyote still sings in the starry night,
and our cousin the spotted cat
yet crouches in the woods.

Be joyful that our grandfather
the mesquite still sends down his long root
to withstand storm and wind,
and that he gives us wood and food.

Be grateful and joyful
that our friends the cactus
and the white bells of yucca
still feed us in the cold months
before our lord's resurrection,
and that our friends the herbs and roots
still give their healing spirits.
Rejoice that our adopted child
with silken tassels and golden ears
now grows in our fields and feeds us.

Be joyful, *xikāwa sāux,*
that when our lord rises from the dead each year,
then also rise the reviving south winds,
then bloom the painted flowers,
then in her earthen den the secretive badger bears her pups,
and then forked-tailed birds flit again in the sweet-scented air.
Be joyful, *xikāwa sāux,*
when we plant seeds in the warming ground.
Have faith that they, too, will rise again.

VI.

wamalēt
after
finally
at last

MANUAL
PARA ADMINISTRAR
LOS SANTOS SACRAMENTOS
DE PENITENCIA,
EUCHARISTIA, EXTREMA-UNCION,
Y MATRIMONIO:

DAR GRACIAS DESPUES DE COMULGAR,
Y AYUDAR A BIEN MORIR

A los Indios de las Naciones: Pajalates, Orejones, Pacaos, Pacóas, Tilijayas, Alasapas, Pausanes, y otras muchas diferentes, que se hallan en las Missiones del Rio de San Antonio, y Rio Grande, pertenecientes à el Colegio de la Santissima Cruz de la Ciudad de Queretaro, como son: Los Pacuàches, Mescales, Pampôpas, Tàcames, Chayopines, Venados, Pamaques, y toda la Juventud de Pihuiques, Borrados, Sanipaos, y Manos de Perro.

COMPUESTO
POR EL P. Fr. BARTHOLOME GARCIA,
Predicador Apostolico, y actual Missionero de la Mission de N. S. P. S. Francisco de dicho Colegio, y Rio de San Antonio, en la Provincia de Texas.

Impresso con las Licencias necessarias en la Imprenta de los Herederos de Doña Maria de Rivera, en la Calle de San Bernardo, y esquina de la Plazuela de el Volador. Año de 1760.

All the dead
Apaxumātz tupāt

We were many—

xotāl
a father's sister

āpxaic t'ān
a daughter of an elder sister

xuē
a woman's son

āptāx āi,
an older brother-in-law

tāyagū
a wife

hā
a child of a son

kāka
a father's mother

kuān
a mother's father

tcāl
a mother's younger sister

k'āu
a husband

And me?
I was a little girl, *t'āwalam can.*

I knew nothing soft in my short life
until I was laid in the satin-lined box
the priests kept for innocents
such as me—a few moments
in finery before I was removed
and buried with the rest of us.

And now, are my eyes shut,
or are they opened?

What do you believe we are?

We who are all the dead,
apaxumātz tupāt.

Do you believe we are
JesuChristo tupōt apkuām sal tupā,
those who are waiting on Jesus Christ?

What I can tell you is,
from the soil of our bodies
green things may grow.

Finding Pieces of the Coahuiltecan World in Words from the Past

Imagine walking in the countryside of southern Texas. It's early morning. The dirt of the field or road is damp, and the slanting light of the early hour throws even the smallest pebble or wisp of grass into sharp relief. A thin but bright rippled edge and its twin shadow catch your eye, and bending down, you gently release a single, shaped stone from its soil bed. You rub the dirt off with your thumb and flip it into the palm of your hand.

Lucky find. Unbroken by any plow, the stone has kept its finely beveled edges and four delicate points: a sharp tip, a pair of barbed shoulders, and a tapered stem that once fastened to a cane shaft. The slender outline of the point is almost iconic, the shape of an arrow drawn by a child as a pointer.

In fact, the stone is a kind of pointer. What you hold in your hand is an arrow that points to another world. You may know the name of the point, Perdiz, assigned to it by archeologists. You may guess the source of the stone, perhaps the gravel bars of the upper Nueces River or the Rio Grande. You may know how the point was made, or have made something like it yourself, painstakingly, with hammerstone and antler. You may know something of the hunter-gatherer culture that produced it. Yet the point itself remains an object of wonder. What was the name of the person, man or woman, who made it? Did it hit its mark? What words might have been said before or after it was launched into flight from the bow? And, what was the world like when it was made?

The indigenous words in this book of poems are also objects of wonder from another world. That world is so remote from us today we cannot even say precisely who lived in it. We cannot understand, precisely, the language they spoke, though some words and phrases survived the passage of time and translators. Even the title of this volume is an uncertainty. Did the word *xuāi* mean "mission," or "house," or "village," as recorded by translators, or something for which we have no exact English word? We often call the people who lived in this world "Coahuiltecans," but this name is an invention and a simplification.

The land between the Sierra Madre Oriental of Mexico and the Balcones Escarpment of Texas once stretched unbroken by any fixed human boundary. It was a sprawling flat patchwork of dense brush, riparian woods, and vast grasslands, broiled by heat in the summer, swept by surprisingly icy winds in winter, and occasionally deluged by floods. In such a harsh land, the indigenous peoples lived lightly and, at times, precariously. They shared a similar way of life: hunting, fishing, and gathering what food they could, traveling only by foot or canoe, and carrying or making on the spot simple tools of stone or bone, antler or wood, or matting, basketry, twine, and hides. When Spanish-speakers first began exploring this land, they found many different small bands of people, to which the Spanish recorded or assigned a welter of names: Pajalates, Alasapas, Orejones, and so on. Some of these various bands of people, however, apparently spoke or understood a common language, a lingua franca. But without books or writing, the words of this language were as fleeting as a cool breeze in the summer—spoken, sung, murmured, recited, or thought, but not recorded.

In a process of centuries, however, some of those spoken words became objects, permanent things of ink and paper: first, probably scrivened with a turkey-feather quill on paper; later stamped into print with a heavy metal press; still later figuratively stamped with the scholarly label of "Coahuilteco."

Franciscan missionaries probably first put these indigenous words to paper, as an aid to evangelizing their speakers. We might pause to imagine one of these Franciscan priests at his task, on the frontier of the civilized world (as he knew it), and, unwittingly, on the frontier of what we might call today *immersive* language learning. We cannot see his face, but we imagine the patched and rough robe, the monastic tonsure, and just below the fringe of hair, the keen ears, upon which broke wave after wave of unfamiliar words spoken by the people around him every day: men, women, children, elderly, speaking in every conceivable tone and timbre. From this free flow of sounds, the missionary eventually understood, separated, processed, and captured pieces of this language. The pieces he thought most important, and only those, he put into the abstract shapes of the Latin alphabet. He wrote them down on paper supplied by the Spanish crown, which supported the missionary efforts to convert the indigenous people to Christian, peaceful, productive, and settled citizens of the realm.

Who was the first to write these words? Impossible to know, given the rare survivals of printed material from the era and the region. Perhaps the Franciscan Gabriel de Vergara, who wrote in 1732 from a San Antonio mission, *El Cuadernillo de la lengua de los indios Pajalates de la Misión de la Purísima Concepción,* a "booklet of the language of the Pajalates Indians of the Mission Purísima Concepción." Amazingly, this early manuscript survived because it became a binding for another, longer document, one which has been the lodestone for studies of this language.

At another San Antonio mission, San Francisco de la Espada, the Franciscan priest named Bartholomé García composed *Manual para administrar los santos sacramentos de penitencia, eucharistia, extrema-uncion, y matritmonio.* Over eighty pages, the *Manual* gave instructions to other Franciscan missionaries on how to administer Catholic sacraments of penitence, eucharist, extreme unction, and marriage—in the language of the people being evangelized. García laid out the manual with side-by-side instructions in Spanish and a language intelligible to various indigenous peoples "which are in the missions of the Río San Antonio, and Río Grande." On the title page he named some of these groups: Pajalates, Orejones, Pacaos, Pacóas, Tilijayas,

Alasapas, Pausanes, Pacuâches, Mescâles, Pampôpas, Tâcames, Chayopînes, Venados, Pamâques, Pihuiques, Borrados, Sanipaos, Manos de Perro, and "many others."

A press in Mexico City committed García's *Manual* to print in 1760. How many copies might have made their way to other Franciscans, zealously laboring on the remote northern frontier of New Spain? How were the Spanish words received by the Indians? How did the missionaries' pronunciation of native words sound to the Indians? How many pages of the *Manual* might have been dog-eared in repeated use, which phrases firmly underscored by a thick thumbnail as vitally important?

Not quite 200 years later García's work and words reappear in a new form. By this time, this lingua franca of so many people had been dubbed "Coahuilteco" by a Mexican scholar. Now, John R. Swanton, an anthropologist working for the Smithsonian Institution, took García's *Manual* and from it parsed a phrase book and vocabulary of Coahuilteco words. Swanton's work appears as a 1940 publication of the Bureau of American Ethnology, "Linguistic Material from the Tribes of Southern Texas and Northeastern Mexico." In the process of creating his phrasebook, Swanton changed some of the spelling to conform to contemporary practice. Even with these changes, however, the words force us to look at the beauty and strangeness of letters and their shapes and sequences on a page, the marvel of sounds and ideas becoming objects through the written or printed word.

Consider García's word

japasc'átzáugt'am

It becomes Swanton's word

xapask'ātzāuxt'am

What does the object of this printed word look like to you? What do you make of the opening slash of the *j* or *x,* the long crowd of rounded *a*'s, the splitting wedges of the apostrophes, the ripple of the ending *m*?

According to Swanton, *xapask'ātzāuxt'am* means "your dreams," or "what you dreamed." In García's *Manual*, we find

bilingual instructions for a Franciscan priest to ask:
> *Has creído lo que suenas?*
> *Japasc'átzáugt'am tuchêm mamayáspámo jam é?*

And in English: "Have you believed your dreams?"

But in the surrounding text of the 1760 *Manual*, a Franciscan is not asking the Indian whether he is idealistically faithful to his life goals. Instead, he is asking whether the Indian has been misled by demons, who might speak to him or her in the form of dreams, or the call of an owl or other bird. How would a Borrado or Pajalates or Pacaos person, whose name we do not know, have answered this question? And how might some of those words have been used in other ways, in other conversations or thoughts?

Like flint flakes and points scattered at a prehistoric campsite, the words are incomplete traces and patterns of the people who spoke them. There are some facts known and much that is unknown about the Coahuilteco speakers, as well as the broader hunter-gatherer cultures of the region, geographically labeled as "Coahuiltecan." The various peoples left no written record of themselves, though they carved and painted images in rock shelters. Such shelters sometimes preserved fragments of the people's belongings, pieces of hide, twine, or basketry, but mostly only stone or bone tools survived the region's withering climate. The earliest Europeans who encountered the peoples of the region, such as famed shipwreck survivor Cabeza de Vaca, wrote relatively thin accounts of the native people they met.

In modern times the story of the various bands of people in the region has been unearthed, assembled, and told by anthropologists, archeologists, and historians such as Thomas N. Campbell, Thomas R. Hester, Martin Salinas, and others. The work of these scholars should be read for their rigorous study of the known pieces of the Coahuiltecan world. The names of some of the many bands of people; some of their cultural practices (that varied between bands) such as tattooing or dancing or peyote use; their material culture that included stone tools, baskets, shells ornaments, and occasional trade goods of obsidian or green stone from remote lands; their food that included snails and snakes and seeds along with deer and rabbit. But at the end of the day, as Martin Salinas concluded in his study, *Indians of the Rio Grande Delta,* "the recorded information on [these] Indian cultures is too scant for fruitful analysis."

But lack of ample evidence does not mean that Coahuiltecan life is now entirely extinct or irrelevant. Perhaps most importantly, descendants of Coahuiltecan peoples live today. Some have carried knowledge of their indigenous heritage over generations; some have rediscovered it. Taking their name from words for "people" or "human beings," *pilam,* and "world" or "earth," *tap,* some of these descendants have joined in groups such as the Tap Pilam Coahuiltecan Nation. And because Indians evangelized by García and other Franciscan priests took Christian names and became Spanish-speakers, there are other people living today who may unknowingly be descendants of Coahuiltecans.

Besides the heritage transmitted through the double helix of human genes, other more visible parts of the Coahuiltecan world still exist. The large owl, or *taxklaxpõ,* still calls hauntingly in the night. White-tailed deer still browse in the woods. The prickly pear cactus and the mesquite have passed into the recipes and *caseros remedios* or home remedies we use today.

But consider what must be lost or missing from the Coahuiltecan world. Societies without writing carry much of their culture in the spoken words—chants or songs, jokes, poems or recitations, stories and myths, rules or prohibitions, deep genealogies, recounted dreams. These are lost. Names and nicknames, curses and endearments. These are gone. And just as tragically, much of the natural world that the Coahuiltecan peoples knew is also gone or threatened. The jaguar and jaguarundi no longer roam the brushland of Texas. Few people today have witnessed the swooping aerial pursuit of an aplomado falcon, and herds of pronghorn no longer roam vast prairies.

In the empty space of what is missing or unknown, I took the liberty to imagine and to create. Neither García, the focused missionary, nor Swanton, the objective scientist, recorded any personal response to the Coahuilteco words they captured, wrote, and studied. But for me—some 75 years after Swanton, over 250 years after García—these written words were my lucky finds, my prized Perdiz or Caracara arrowheads. Even from the battered and browned copy of Swanton's study that I purchased for a few dollars, the words leapt out as beautiful, delicate, sharp, eloquent yet tantalizing. They launched me into imaginative flight about the people who once spoke them. Imaginative, and I hope, empathetic.

Each poem in this volume presents the imagined words or thoughts of a different Coahuilteco speaker, and each poem includes some of the Coahuilteco words and phrases recorded by García and Swanton. In some poems, the words are used as they would have been spoken by Franciscans using the *Manual*. In others, I have taken the words and given them back to the indigenous people for their own use, different from the way they are used in the *Manual*. Speaking from the poems are adults, children, elders, youths, men and women. All of them live in or near one of the Spanish missions in what is now southern Texas or northeastern Mexico.

Although there are whole realms of life not touched on by the García / Swanton vocabulary—hunting, cooking, child-rearing, daydreaming, much of the material world, and the entirety of indigenous life before contact with western culture—the words from this mission period are crucial. Franciscan missionaries labored for over a century in the region, from the late 1600s to the first decades of the 1800s. For those indigenous people who did not die of disease or combat, who were not enslaved and removed from the area, who did not flee to more remote or inaccessible lands, a Spanish mission became the crucible of contact between them, people of other bands who were also collected there, and the new Spanish-speaking culture. Some might argue that the Spanish mission was also the anvil over which indigenous cultures were hammered into a new, almost unrecognizable form. Others main-

tain that the missions and the Franciscan priests offered salvation for indigenous people, who were already beset by European-born disease, hunger, encroachment by other tribes such as the Apache or Comanche, exploitation by colonists or soldiers, and the inevitable advance of western culture.

And just as there are differing views today on the role of the missions and the people they evangelized, so there are different speakers and opinions in these poems. Surely Coahuilteco speakers, or any indigenous persons who entered a mission, brought their own private history and memory, observations, prejudices, fears, hopes, and beliefs. Each was an individual actor in history not yet made.

The people who once spoke to Fray García could not have known that some of their language's words would reach us, in such piecemeal and round-about fashion, over two hundred years later. If they had, what words would they have most wanted to leave us? What would they have wanted to say about their life? Perhaps this:

Apkuētukuē apāxāi santcē wasāyaxām,
It will never be extinguished.

Lisa Kay Adam

www.ingramcontent.com/pod-product-compliance
Lightning Source LLC
Chambersburg PA
CBHW071232090426
42736CB00014B/3055